COMPANY LAW

Mastering Essential Legal Terms Explained About Limited Liability Companies, Joint-Stock Companies, Partnership, Private Enterprises, And Groups of Companies.

DR. PETER JOHNSON

ISBN: 9798672253527

Table of Contents

INTRODUCTION

Thank you and congratulate you for downloading the book *"COMPANY LAW: Mastering Essential Legal Terms Explained About Limited Liability Companies, Joint-Stock Companies, Partnership, Private Enterprises, And Groups of Companies!"*

With a clear, concise, engaging writing and sophisticated analysis style, Dr. Peter Johnson will help you with a practical understanding of the ever-changing landscape of business and company law covering corporate structure, corporate governance, corporate finance, and corporate rescue and restructuring; provide you a road map to navigating enterprises rules of Limited Liability Companies, Joint-Stock Companies, Partnership, Private Enterprises, Groups of Companies and help you build a foundation for understanding the overall picture and much much more. This book delivers extensive coverage of every aspect of the law and details the duties a paralegal is expected to perform when working within business and company law. High-level, comprehensive coverage is combined with cutting-edge developments and foundational concepts.

As the author of the book, I promise this book will be an invaluable source of legal reference for professionals, international lawyers, law students, business professionals and anyone else who want to improve their use of legal terminology, succinct clarification of legal terms and have a better understanding of business and company law. This book provides you with a comprehensive and highly practical approach in legal contexts, the world of enterprises rules related Limited Liability Companies, Joint-Stock Companies, Partnership, Private Enterprises, Groups of Companies. All legal terms and phrases are well written and explained clearly in plain English.

Thank you again for purchasing this book, and I hope you enjoy it.

Let's get started!

EXPLANATION OF TERMS

Shareholder means any individual or organization that owns at least one share issued by a joint-stock company.

Dividend means the net profit in terms of money or asset paid to the owner of each share from residual profit of the joint-stock company after all financial obligations are fulfilled.

Enterprise means an economic organization that has its own name, assets, stable transaction office and has been lawfully registered for the purpose of conducting business.

Permanent address means the address of the head office of an organization, permanent residence address or office address or any other address of an individual that is registered with the enterprise as contact address;

Market price of the capital contribution or share means the transactional price in the security market or price defined by a professional valuation organization.

Certificate of Business registration means a paper or electronic file issued by the business registration authority to the enterprise which contains information about business registration.

Capital contribution means the contribution of assets to form the company's charter capital.

Business means the continuous implementation of one, several or all of stages of an investment process such as manufacturing, selling products or services on the market to earn profit.

Founder means any organization or individual that establishes or contributes capital to establish an enterprise.

Foreign investor means any organization or individual that is defined as a foreign investor according to Law.

Stake means the total value of assets that a member/partner contributes or promises to contribute to a company. Stake holding means the ratio of a member/partner's stake to charter capital of the company.

Enterprise restructuring is either a total division, partial division, consolidation, acquisition of an enterprise, or conversion of the type of business entity.

Foreign organization means any organization that is established overseas under another country's law.

Charter capital means the total value of assets that are contributed or promised to be contributed by members/partners when establishing a limited liability company or partnership; or the total face value of shares that are sold or registered when establishing a joint-stock company.

Enterprise manager means the owner, director of a private enterprise, general partner of a partnership, chairman of the Members' Council, president of the company, member of the Management Board, director or general director or another important managerial position provided for in the company's charter.

Authorized representative means an individual who is authorized in writing by a member organization of a limited liability company or a shareholder-organization of a joint-stock company to exercise its rights in the company in accordance with the provisions of this Law.

Restructuring of an enterprise means the separation, division, consolidation, merger or transformation of an enterprise.

Market price of the capital contribution or share means the transactional price in the security market or price defined by a professional valuation organization.

Nationality of an enterprise means the nationality of a country or territory where such an enterprise is established and registered.

Permanent address means the address of the head office of an organization, permanent residence address or office address or any other address of an individual that is registered with the enterprise as contact address;

RIGHTS OF ENTERPRISES

1. To enjoy business autonomy; take initiative in choosing business lines, localities, and forms of business and investment; take initiative in expanding business in terms of size and business line; to be encouraged, given incentives, and facilitated by the State to produce or provide public products or services.

2. To choose forms and methods of raising and using capital.

3. To take initiative in the search for markets, customers, and in signing contracts.

4. To conduct import and export business.

5. To recruit, hire and use laborers to meet business requirements.

6. To apply, on their own initiative, modern science and technology in order to raise business efficiency and competitiveness.

7. To enjoy autonomy in deciding on business affairs and internal relations.

8. To possess, use and dispose of their assets.

9. To deny any requests for supply of resources that are not provided for by law.

10. To lodge complaints and denunciations in accordance with the law on complains and denunciations.

11. To participate in legal proceedings directly or via authorized representatives.

THE COMPANY'S CHARTER

The company's charter consists:

a) Name, address of the headquarter of the enterprise; names, addresses of its branches and representative office (if any);

b) Business lines;

c) Capital share and the value of contributed capital by each member, for limited liability companies or partnerships; total shares, types of shares, and nominal values of each type of shares if the enterprise is a joint-stock company;

d) Rights and obligations of members in limited liability companies or partnerships; of shareholders in joint-stock companies.

e) Management organizational structure.

f) The representative-at-law, for limited liability companies or joint-stock companies.

g) Formalities for approval of decisions of the company; principles for the settlement of internal disputes.

h) Bases and methods to decide on remuneration, salaries and bonuses for managers and members of the Control Board or controllers.

i) Principles for distribution of after-tax profit and handling of losses.

k) Cases of dissolution and procedures for dissolution and liquidation of assets of the company.

l) Formalities for amending and supplementing the company's charter.

CONTRIBUTED ASSETS

1. Contributed assets may be local currencies, convertible foreign currencies, gold, value rights to use land, the value of intellectual property rights, technologies, technical secrets, and other assets.

2. Intellectual property rights contributed as capital include copyrights and relevant rights, industrial property rights, plant variety rights, and other intellectual property rights prescribed by regulations of law on intellectual property. Only the organizations and individuals who are legitimate owners of the aforementioned rights may contribute such assets as capital.

TRANSFER OF PROPERTY OWNERSHIP

1. Members of limited liability companies or partnerships, and shareholders of joint-stock companies must transfer ownership of assets used to make capital contribution to the companies according to the following provisions:

a) For assets of which ownership has been registered or for land-use rights, capital contributors shall have to carry out procedures for transferring ownership of such assets or land-use rights to the companies at a competent state agency.

Transfer of ownership of assets used to make capital contribution shall not be subject to registration fee;

b) For assets of which ownership is not required to register, they shall be contributed in the form of asset delivery and receipt certified by a written minute.

The delivery and receipt minutes must clearly state: name and address of the company's head office; full name, permanent address, nationality, number of the people's identity card, passport or other lawful personal certification, number of the establishment decision or business registration certificate of the capital contributor; types of assets, quantity of assets of each type, total value of assets and its proportion in the company's charter capital; date of asset delivery and receipt and signature of the capital contributor or his/her authorized representative and the representative-at-law of the company;

c) Shares or capital shares that are not paid in the local currency, freely convertible foreign currency and gold shall be regarded as fully paid when ownership of assets used to make capital contribution is lawfully transferred to the company.

2. Private enterprise owners shall not be required to carry out procedures for transferring ownership of their own assets used in business operation to their enterprises.

Assessing Contributed Assets

Contributed assets other than local currencies, gold, freely convertible foreign currency, the value of intellectual property rights, the value of land use rights, technology, or other types of assets must be assessed by members/general partners, founding shareholders, or professional valuation organizations and stated in the company's charter.

HEAD OFFICES OF ENTERPRISES

The head office of an enterprise is a location where it is situated in, with an address, which consists of the house number, street, commune, district, province, phone number, fax number, and email address (if any).

THE ENTERPRISE SEAL

1. Every enterprise shall have its own seal. Enterprises must keep and preserve their seals at their head offices. The design and contents of seals, conditions for making seals and regulations on seal usage shall comply with regulations of the Government.

2. The seal is a property of an enterprise. The representative-at-law of an enterprise must be responsible for managing the use of its seal in accordance with the provisions of law.

BRANCHES, REPRESENTATIVE OFFICES, AND BUSINESS LOCATIONS OF THE ENTERPRISE

1. A branch is an affiliated unit of an enterprise and is tasked to perform all or some functions of such enterprise, including acting as an authorized representative. Business lines of branches must be consistent with those of their enterprises.

2. A representative office is an affiliated unit of an enterprise and is authorized to act on behalf of the enterprise to protect its interests. The organization and operation of representative offices shall comply with the provisions of law.

3. Business location is a place where an enterprise carries out its business activities.

4. Branches, representative offices and business locations of the enterprises must bear the names of the enterprises supplemented with indications of such branches, representative offices or business locations.

Establishment of Branches, Representative Offices

Every enterprise is entitled to establish a branch or representative office, whether at home or overseas. An enterprise may establish one or multiple branches/representative offices in an administrative division.

LIMITED LIABILITY COMPANY

LIMITED LIABILITY COMPANIES WITH TWO OR MORE MEMBERS

A limited liability company with two or more members is an enterprise of which:

Members are responsible for debts and other property liabilities of the enterprise within the amount of capital that they have committed to contribute to the enterprise.

Rights of Members

Members of a limited liability company with two or more members shall have the following rights:

1. Participate in meetings of the Board of members; discuss, propose, make suggestions and vote on the issues within the competence of the Board of members.

2. Cast a number of votes that is proportional to the member's stake.

3. Receive a proportion of profits that is proportional to the member's stake after the company has fully paid taxes and fulfilled other financial obligations according to law;

4. Receive a proportion of remaining assets that is proportional to the member's stake after the company is dissolved or goes bankrupt.

5. Has the preemptive right to contribute additional capital when the company's charter capital is increased.

6. Dispose of his/her own stake by transfer, bequeath, donation or otherwise according to the provisions of law and the company's charter;

Obligations of Member

1. Contribute capital fully and punctually; take liability for the debts and other liabilities of the company up to the value of capital contributed.

2. Do not withdraw contributed capital in any shape or form.

3. Comply with the company's charter.

4. Comply with resolutions and decisions of the Board of members.

5. To be liable individually when acting on behalf of the company to:

a) Violate the laws;

b) Conduct business or other transactions not in the interest of the company but causing damage to other persons;

c) Pay off undue debts when there is a financial danger facing the company.

Organizational Structure

A limited liability company with two or more members has a Board of members, a Chairperson of the Board of members, a Director/General Director.

1. The Board of members consists of all company's members and is the highest decision-making body of the company.

2. The Board of members has the following rights and obligations:

a) To decide on the development strategy and annual business plans of the company;

b) To decide on the increase or decrease of the charter capital, time and methods for mobilizing capital;

c) To decide on methods of investment and investment projects of the company;

d) To elect, remove or dismiss the chairman of the Members' Council; decide to appoint, remove, dismiss, sign or terminate contracts with the director or general director, chief accountant and other managers as provided for in the company's charter;

e) To decide on salaries, bonuses and other benefits of the director or general director, chief accountant and other managers as provided for in the company's charter;

f) To adopt annual financial statements and plans for using or distributing profits as well as handling losses of the company;

g) To decide on the management organization structure of the company;

h) To decide on opening of subsidiary companies, branches and/or representative offices;

i) To amend and/or supplement the company's charter;

j) To decide on the company's reorganization;

k) To decide on dissolution or bankruptcy of the company;

Authorized Representatives

1. The authorized representative must satisfy the following criteria and conditions:

a) Having full civil act capacity;

b) Not being prohibited from establishing and managing an enterprise;

c) Having professional qualifications and experience in business management or in the major business line of the company;

2. The authorized representative shall act on behalf of the authorizing member in exercising all rights and performing all obligations of a member of the Board of members.

Chairperson Of The Board Of Members

1. The Board of members shall elect a member as the Chairperson. The Chairperson of the Board of members may concurrently hold the position of the company's Director/General Director.

2. The Chairperson of the Board of members has the following rights and obligations:

a) Prepare the agenda and operation plan of the Board of members;

b) Prepare the agenda, contents, documents of meetings of the Board of members or for absentee voting;

c) Convene and chair meetings of the Board of members or organize the absentee voting;

d) Carry out or organize supervision of implementation of Resolutions of the Board of members;

e) Sign Resolutions of the Board of members on behalf of the Board of members;

Minutes of meetings of the Board of members

1. Meetings of the Board of members must be recorded in writing, audio recordings, or other electronic media of recordings.

2. The minutes of the meeting must be completed and passed before the end of the meeting. The minutes must have the following content:

a) Time, location, purposes, agenda of the meeting;

b) Full names, proportions of stakes, numbers and issuance dates of certificates of capital contribution of members or authorized representatives of members that attend the meeting; Full names, proportions of stakes, numbers and issuance dates of certificates of capital contribution of members or authorized representatives of members that do not attend the meetings;

c) The issues discussed and voted; summary opinions of members about each issue;

d) A total number of valid votes, invalid votes, affirmative votes, and negative votes for each issue.

e) The decisions ratified;

f) Full names and signatures of the minute's maker and the chair of the meeting.

Director/General Director

1. The Director or General Director of a company is the person who administers the everyday business operation of the company and is responsible to the Board of members for the performance of his/her rights and obligations.

2. The Director/General Director has the following rights and obligations:

a) Organize the implementation of Resolutions of the Board of members;

b) Decide the issues related to the company's everyday business operation;

c) Organize the implementation of the company's business plans and investment plans;

d) Promulgate the company's rules and regulations, unless otherwise prescribed by the company's charter;

e) Designate, dismiss the company's managerial positions, except for those within the competence of the Board of members;

f) Sign contracts on behalf of the company, except for those within the competence of the Board of members;

g) Propose organizational structure plan;

h) Submit annual financial statements to the Board of members;

i) Propose plans for use of profits or loss settlement;

Adjustment To Charter Capital

1. The company may increases its charter capital in the following cases:

a) Capital contribution of members is increased;

b) Capital contributions are made by new members.

2. When increasing stakes of members, the additional capital shall be split to the members according to their proportion of stakes to the company's charter capital.

Conditions For Profit Distribution

The company shall only distribute profits to its members when its business operation is profitable, tax liability and other financial obligations are fulfilled in accordance with law, debts and other liabilities can be paid after profit distribution.

One-Member Limited Liability Company

1. A one-member limited liability company is an enterprise under the ownership of an organization or individual (hereinafter referred to as the company's owner; the company's owner is liable for the company's debts and other liabilities up to the company's charter capital.

2. A one-member limited liability company has its legal status from the issuance date of the Certificate of Business registration.

Capital Contribution To The Company's Establishment

1. Charter capital of a one-member limited liability company on the business registration date is the total value of assets promised to be contributed by the owner, which is written in the company's charter.

2. The owner, with his/her entire property, shall take responsibility for the company's financial obligations, the damage caused by failure to contribute capital, or failure to fully and punctually contribute capital.

The Board Of Members

Members of the Board of members shall be designated and dismissed by the company's owner. The Board of members, on behalf of the company, shall perform rights and obligations of the company's owner and the company; take legal responsibility to the company's owner for the fulfillment of rights and obligations in accordance with regulations of law.

The Company's President

The company's President is designated by the owner. The company's President, on behalf of the company's owner, shall perform rights and obligations of the company's owner and the company, except for rights and obligations of the Director/General Director; take legal responsibility to the company's owner for the fulfillment of rights and obligations in accordance with regulations of law, and the company's charter.

Rights of the Company Owner

1. The company owner that is an organization shall have following rights:

a) To decide on contents of the company's charter and its amendment or supplement;

b) To decide on the development strategy and annual business plan of the company;

c) To decide on the structure of organization and management; appoint, remove from office and dismiss managers of the company;

d) To approve investment projects valued at 50% or more of total value of assets recorded in the latest financial statement of the company or a smaller percentage as provided for in the company's charter;

e) To decide on methods of market development, marketing and technology;

f) To approve lending, borrowing and other contracts as provided for in the company's charter which are valued at 50% or more of total value of assets recorded in the latest financial statement of the company or at a smaller percentage as provided for in the company's charter;

g) To decide on sale of assets valued at 50% or more of total value of assets recorded in the latest financial statement of the company or at a smaller percentage as provided for in the company's charter;

h) To decide on increase of the charter capital; transfer of part or whole of the charter capital of the company to another organization or individual;

i) To decide on setting up subsidiaries and making capital contribution to other companies;

j) To conduct supervision and evaluation of business performance of the company;

k) To decide on use of profits after fulfilling tax and other financial obligations of the company;

l) To decide on re-organization, dissolution and request for bankruptcy of the company;

m) To collect the whole value of assets of the company after it finishes the dissolution or bankruptcy process;

2. The company owner that is an individual shall have following rights:

a) To decide on contents of the company's charter and its amendment or supplement;

b) To decide on investment and business activities and internal management of the company, unless otherwise provided for in the company's charter;

c) To transfer part or whole of the charter capital of the company to another organization or individual;

d) To decide on use of profits after fulfilling tax and other financial obligations of the company;

e) To decide on re-organization, dissolution and request for bankruptcy of the company;

f) To collect the whole value of assets of the company after it finishes the dissolution or

Obligations of the Company Owner

1. To make capital contribution fully and on time as committed; if not, to be liable for all debts and other property liabilities of the company;

2. To observe the company's charter;

3. To keep assets of the company and company owner separated;

The company owner who is an individual must separate between the expenditure of himself or herself and that of the company owner or director or general director.

4. To observe laws on contracts and relevant laws on sale, purchase, borrowing, lending, lease, renting or other transactions between the company and the company owner.

President of The Company

1. The president of the company shall act on behalf of the company owner in exercising his/her rights and performing his/her obligations: act on behalf of the company in exercising its rights and performing its obligations; be responsible to the company owner in exercising assigned rights and duties.

2. Specific rights, obligations and duties and working regime of the president of the company toward the company owner shall comply with the company's charter.

3. Decisions of the president of the company on exercise of rights and performance of obligations of the company owner shall be legally effective from the date of approval by the company owner.

Director or General Director

1. The director or general director shall run day-to-day business operation of the company and be responsible to the president of the company in exercising his/her rights and duties.

2. The director or general director shall have following powers:

a) To organize implementation of decisions of the president of the company;

b) To decide on matters related to day-to-day business operation of the company;

c) To organize implementation of business and investment plans of the company;

d) To issue internal management regulations of the company;

e) To appoint, remove and dismiss managers in the company, except those falling under the competence of the president of the company;

f) To conclude contracts on behalf of the company, except those falling under the competence of president of the company;

g) To make proposals on the organizational structure of the company;

h) To submit annual financial settlement reports to the president of the company;

i) To make proposal on distribution of profits or settlement of losses;

j) To recruit laborers;

3. The director or general director must meet the following qualifications and conditions:

a) Having full civil act capacity;

b) Not being prohibited from managing an enterprise in accordance with regulations of law;

c) Having relevant expertise and experience in business management or major business line of the company; or meeting other qualifications and conditions as provided for in the company's charter.

JOINT-STOCK COMPANIES

Joint-Stock Companies

A joint-stock company is an enterprise where:

a) Its charter capital is split into multiple units of equal value called shares;

b) Shareholders may be organizations and individuals; the minimum number of shareholders shall be three; the maximum number shall not be restricted.

c) Shareholders are only liable for the enterprise's debts and other liabilities within the limit of the value of their capital contribution to the enterprise;

Capital of Joint-Stock Companies

1. Charter capital of a joint-stock company is to total face value of sold shares.

2. Sold shares are a number of authorized shares that have been paid-off by shareholders to the company.

3. Authorized shares are the total amount of shares of various types that the General Meeting of Shareholders decides to offer to raise capital.

4. Unsold shares are authorized shares that have not been paid-off. On the enterprise registration date, unsold shares are the total amount of shares that are not registered by shareholders.

Types of Shares

1. A joint-stock company must issue ordinary shares. Holders of ordinary shares are called ordinary shareholders.

2. Apart from ordinary shares, A joint-stock company may issue preference shares. Holders of preference shares are called preference shareholders.

Preference shares include:

a) Voting preference shares;

b) Dividend preference shares;

c) Redeemable preference shares;

Rights of Ordinary Shareholders

1. Every ordinary shareholder is entitled to:

a) Attend and give opinions at the General Meetings of Shareholders; exercise the right to vote directly or via an authorized representative or in another form permitted by law or the company's charter.

b) Receive dividends at a rate decided by the General Meeting of Shareholders;

c) Be given priority in buying newly-offered shares in proportion to his/her ordinary shares;

d) Freely transfer their shares to other shareholders and those who are other than shareholders.

e) Examine and collect information from the List of shareholders having voting right; request adjustments to incorrect information;

f) Examine, copy the company's charter, minutes of General Meeting of Shareholders, and Resolutions of the General Meeting of Shareholders;

g) Receive a proportion of remaining asset which is proportional to his/her holdings when the company is dissolved or bankrupt.

Rights of Ordinary Shareholders

1. Pay for the ordered shares fully and punctually.

Do not withdraw capital contributed by ordinary shares in any shape or form, unless such shares are repurchased by the company or other persons.

2. Comply with the company's charter, rules and regulations.

3. Comply with Resolutions of the General Meeting of Shareholders and the Board of Directors.

4. Fulfill other obligations prescribed in the company's charter.

Obligations of Ordinary Shareholders

1. Pay for the ordered shares fully and punctually.

Do not withdraw capital contributed by ordinary shares in any shape or form, unless such shares are repurchased by the company or other persons.

2. Comply with the company's charter, rules and regulations.

3. Comply with Resolutions of the General Meeting of Shareholders and the Board of Directors.

4. Fulfill other obligations prescribed in the company's charter.

Voting Preference Shares

Voting preference shares are the shares with more votes than ordinary shares; the number of votes of a voting preference share shall be prescribed by the company's charter.

Shares With Preferred Dividends And Rights Of Holders Thereof

Shares with preferred dividends are shares that pay higher dividends than dividends of ordinary shares, or that pay a fixed amount of annual dividends. Annual distributed dividends include fixed dividend and bonus dividends; fixed dividend does not depend on the company's business outcome.

Redeemable Preferred Shares

Redeemable preferred shares are shares that will be redeemed by the company at the request of their holders or under the conditions written thereon.

Share Certificates

Share certificates are certificates issued by a joint-stock company, book entries, or electronic data which certify ownership of one or an amount of shares of the company. A share certificate must contain the following information:

a) Name, ID number, headquarter address of the enterprise;

b) Amount and type of shares;

c) Face value of each share and total face value of shares written on the share certificate;

d) Full name, address, Nationality, ID)passport number if the shareholder is an individual; name, enterprise identification number or establishment decision number, and headquarter address if the shareholder is an organization;

Shareholder Register

1. Every joint-stock company shall make and keep the shareholder register from the issuance date of the Certificate of Business registration. The shareholder register may be paper documents, electronic data, or both.

2. The shareholder register must contain the following information:

a) Name, headquarter address of the company;

b) Total number of authorized shares, types of authorized shares, and number of each type of authorized shares;

c) Total sold shares of each type and value of contributed share capital;

d) Full name, permanent address, nationality, number of the people's identity card, passport or other lawful personal certification of the shareholder being an individual; name, permanent address, nationality, number of the establishment decision or business registration certificate of the shareholder being in an organization;

e) The amount of each type of shares held by each shareholder; date of shares registration.

Share Offering

1. Share offering means the company's increase in a number of authorized shares and selling such shares during the company's operation to increase charter capital.

2. Share offering may be carried out in the following forms:

a) Offering of shares to existing shareholders;

b) Public offering of shares;

c) Private placement of shares.

Selling Shares

The Board of Directors shall decide the time, method of sale, and selling prices of shares. Selling prices of shares must not fall below the market price on the offering.

Share Transfer

The transfer shall be made under a common contract or via a transaction on the securities market. Where the transfer is made into a contract, transfer documents must bear the signatures of the transferor and the transferee (or their representatives). Where the transfer is made via a transaction on the securities market, the procedures and recording of ownership shall comply with regulations of law on securities.

Bond Issuance

A joint-stock company is entitled to issue bonds, convertible bonds, and other bonds as prescribed by law and the company's charter.

Purchases Of Shares And Bonds

Shares, bonds of joint-stock companies may be purchased with the local currency unit, convertible foreign currencies, gold, land use right value, the value of intellectual property rights, technologies, technical secrets, and other assets prescribed by the company's charter. The payment shall be made in a lump sum.

Repurchase Of Shares At The Request Of Shareholders

1. Any shareholder who votes against the Resolution on the company's restructuring or changes to the shareholders' rights and obligations prescribed in the company's charter shall be entitled to request the company to repurchase his/her shares. The request shall be made in writing, specifying the shareholder's name, address, the amount of each type of shares, wanted prices, and reasons for requesting the repurchase.

2. The company shall repurchase shares at the request of shareholders at market prices. If an agreement on the price is not reached, both parties may request a professional valuation organization to carry out the valuation. The decision given by such organization shall be final.

Repurchase Of Shares Under The Company's Decision

The company may repurchase the shares held by each shareholder in proportion to his/her holding in the company. In this case, a notification of the decision to repurchase shares must be sent by registered mail to all shareholders within thirty days as from the date of approval of such decision. The notification must contain the name, headquarter address of the company, total amount of shares and types of shares repurchased, repurchase prices or rules for determination of repurchase prices; procedures and deadline for payment; procedures and deadline for shareholders to offer their shares to the company.

Dividend Payment

1. Dividends on preferred shares shall be paid under conditions applied to each type of preferred shares.

2. Dividends on ordinary shares are determined according to the net profit earned and the dividend payment extract from the undistributed profit of the company. A joint-stock company may only pay dividends on ordinary shares when all of the conditions below are satisfied:

a) The company has fulfilled tax liability and other financial obligations as prescribed by law;

b) The company's funds have been established and developed; previous losses are fully offset against as prescribed by law and the company's charter;

c) Right after the dividend is fully paid, the company is still able to pay due debts and other liabilities.

3. Dividends may be paid in cash, the company's shares, or other assets prescribed by the company's charter. If the dividend is paid in cash, the currency shall be the local one; it is permissible to make dividend payment by checks, wire transfer, or payment order by post to the shareholders' permanent residences or mailing addresses.

Organizational Structure Of A Joint-Stock Company

1. Every joint-stock company is entitled to decide whether to organize and operate according to one of the two models below:

a) The General Meeting of Shareholders, the Board of Directors, the Control Board, and the Director/General Director.

b)The General Meeting of Shareholders, the Board of Directors, and the Director/General Director.

2. If there is only one legal representative, the Chairperson of the Board of Directors or the Director/General Director shall be the legal representative; unless otherwise prescribed by the company's charter, the Chairperson of the Board of Directors shall be the legal representative of the company. If there are more than one legal representatives, the Chairperson of the Board of Directors and the Director/General Director shall naturally be the legal representatives of the company.

General Meeting Of Shareholders

1. The General Meeting of Shareholders consists of all shareholders having the voting right and is the supreme regulatory body of a joint-stock company.

2. The General Meeting of Shareholders has the following rights and obligations:

a) Ratify the company's development orientation;

b) Decide the types of shares and amount of each type of authorized shares; decide annual dividend payment of each type of shares;

c) Elect, dismiss, discharge from duty members of the Board of Directors and Controllers;

d) Decide amendments to the company's charter;

e) Ratify annual financial statements;

g) Consider taking actions against violations committed by the Board of Directors and the Control Board that cause damage to the company and its shareholders;

h) Decide the company's restructuring and dissolution;

Power To Convene General Meetings Of Shareholders

An annual general meeting shall be held at least one per year. Apart from annual general meetings, extraordinary general meetings may be held .

The Annual General Meeting of Shareholders shall discuss and ratify the following issues:

a) The company's annual business plan;

b) The annual financial statement;

c) Report of the Board of Directors on business administration and performance of the Board of Directors and each member thereof;

d) Report of the Control Board on the company's business outcome, performance of the Board of Directors, Director/General Director;

e) Self-assessment report of the Control Board and each Controller;

f) Level of dividend on each share of each type;

List Of Shareholders Entitled To Attend General Meeting Of Shareholders

1. The list of shareholders entitled to participate in the General Meeting of Shareholders shall be compiled according to the company's shareholder register.

2. The list of shareholders entitled to participate in a meeting of the General Meeting of Shareholders shall include full name, permanent address, nationality, number of the people's identity card, passport or other lawful personal certification of every shareholder being an individual, or number of the establishment decision or business registration certificate of every shareholder being an organization; quantity of shares of each type; number and date of registration of each shareholder.

3. Shareholders are entitled to inspect, examine, copy the list of shareholders entitled to attend the General Meeting of Shareholders; request adjustment to incorrect information or addition of necessary information about themselves to the list. The company's manager must promptly provide information about in the shareholder register, adjust incorrect information at the request of shareholders; pay compensation for damage caused by failure to provide information or failure to provide timely, accurate information in the shareholder register on request. Procedures for requesting provision of information in the shareholder register shall comply with the company's charter.

Invitation To General Meeting Of Shareholders

1. The convener of the General Meeting of Shareholders shall send invitations to all shareholders on the list of shareholders entitled to attend the General Meeting of Shareholders before the opening date. Every invitation must contain the name, address of the head office, number and date of the business registration certificate, place of business registration of the company; name and permanent address of the shareholder or the shareholder's authorized representative, time and venue of the meeting.

2. Invitations shall be sent by registered mail to mailing addresses of shareholders; the invitation shall also be posted on the company's website according to the company's charter.

3. The invitation shall be enclosed with the following documents:

a) The agenda, documents used during the meeting, and draft resolution on each issue on the agenda;

b) The ballot;

c) The form to appoint authorized representative to attend the meeting.

Minutes Of General Meeting Of Shareholders

1. The General Meeting of Shareholders must be recorded in writing, audio recordings, or other electronic means of recordings. The meeting minutes must has the following information:

a) Name, address of the head office, number and date of grant of the business registration certificate, place of business registration;

b) Time and location of the General Meeting of Shareholders;

c) Agenda and contents of the meeting;

d) Full names of the chair and secretary

e) Summary of the meeting and opinions given at the General Meeting of Shareholders with regard to each issue on the agenda;

f) The number of shareholders and total number of votes of attending shareholders; list of registered shareholders, representatives of shareholders, corresponding amount shares and votes;

g) Total votes on each issue, specifying the voting method, numbers of valid votes, invalid votes, affirmative votes, negative votes; the corresponding ratio to total votes of attending shareholders;

h) The issues ratified and the corresponding ratio of affirmative votes;

i) Signatures of the chair and secretary.

Effect Of Resolutions Of The General Meeting Of Shareholders

A Resolution of the General Meeting of Shareholders is effective from the day on which it is ratified or on the effective date written thereon.

Board Of Directors

1. The Board of Directors is a regulatory body of the company, has the power to, on behalf of the company, make decisions, perform the company's rights and obligations beyond the competence of the General Meeting of Shareholders.

2. The Board of members has the following rights and obligations:

a) Decide the strategies, midterm development plans, and annual business plans of the company;

b) Propose types of shares and total authorized shares of each type;

c) Decide the sale of new shares within the amount of authorized shares of each type; decide to raise additional capital in other manners;

d) Decide selling prices of the company's shares and bonds;

e) Decide repurchases of shares according to the company's charter;

f) Decide investment plans and projects of investment within its competence and limits prescribed by law;

g) Decide solutions for market development, marketing, and technology;

h) Elect, dismiss, discharge from duty the Chairperson of the Board of Directors; designate, dismiss, sign contracts, terminate contracts with the Director/General Director and other key managers prescribed by the company's charter; decide salaries and other benefits of such managers; appoint representative to participate in the Board of members or the General Meeting of Shareholders of another company; decide the wages and other benefits of such persons;

i) Supervise, direct the Director/General Director and other managers to run the company's everyday business operation;

k) Decide the organizational structure, rules and regulations of the company, establishment of subsidiaries, branches, representative office, capital contributions to or purchase of shares of other enterprises;

l) Approve the agenda and documents of the General Meeting of Shareholders, convene the General Meeting of Shareholders or carry out absentee voting for the General Meeting of Shareholders to ratify decisions;

m) Submit annual financial statements to the General Meeting of Shareholders;

n) Propose the level of dividend payment; decide the deadline and procedures for dividend payment or settlement of losses incurred during the business operation;

o) Propose restructuring, dissolution, petition for bankruptcy of the company;

Standards And Conditions For Members Of The Board Of Directors

Members of the Board of Directors must:

a) Be legally competent;

b) Has qualifications and experience of business administration; Members of the Board of Directors are not necessarily shareholders of the company.

Chairperson Of The Board Of Directors

1. The Board of Directors shall elect a member of the Board of Directors as the Chairperson. The Chairperson of the Board of Directors may concurrently hold the position of Director/General Director.

2. The Chairperson of the Board of Directors has the following rights and obligations:

a) Formulate operation plans of the Board of Directors;

b) Prepare the agenda, contents, and documents of meetings; convene and chair meetings of the Board of Directors;

c) Organize the ratification of Resolutions of the Board of Directors;

d) Supervise the implementation of Resolutions of the Board of Directors;

e) Chair meetings of the General Meeting of Shareholders and the Board of Directors;

Meetings Of The Board Of Directors

1. The Board of Directors may hold periodic and extraordinary meetings. The Board of Directors shall hold meetings at the company's headquarter or other locations.

2. Meetings of the Board of Directors shall be held by the Chairperson of the Board of Directors when it is deemed necessary.

3. The Chairperson of the Board of Directors shall convene a meeting of the Board of Directors in the following cases:

a) The meeting is requested by the Control Board or independent members

b) The meeting is requested by the Director/General Director;

The request must be made in writing, specifying the purposes, issues that need discussing, and decisions within the competence of the Board of Directors.

Minutes Of Meetings Of The Board Of Directors

1. Meetings of the Board of Directors shall be recorded in writing, audio recordings, or other electronic means. The minutes must contain the following information:

a) The enterprise's name, enterprise identification number, address of the headquarter;

b) Purposes, agenda, and contents of the meeting;

c) Time and location of the meeting;

d) Full name of each attending member or their authorized person, method of participation; full name of every member that does not attend and explanations;

e) Issues discussed and voted on at the meeting;

f) Summary of opinions of each attending member in chronological order;

g) Voting result, specifying the members that cast affirmative votes, negative votes, and abstentions;

h) The issues that have been ratified;

i) Full names, signatures of the chair and the minute's maker.

Right To Obtain Information Of Members Of The Board Of Directors

1. Members of the Board of Directors are entitled to request the Director/General Director or Deputy Director/Deputy General Director, and managers of units in the company to provide information about the financial status and performance of the company and units in the company.

2. The requested must provide timely, sufficient, accurate information and documents at the request of Members of the Board of Directors. Procedures for requesting and providing information shall be prescribed by the company's charter.

Director/General Director

1. The Board of Directors shall appoint one of them as or hire a Director/General Director.

2. The Director/General Director shall run the company's everyday business, be supervised by the Board of Directors, take responsibility to the Board of Directors for the performance of given rights and obligations.

3. The Director/General Director has the following rights and obligations:

a) Decide important issues related to the company's everyday business without decision of the Board of Directors;

b) Organize the implementation of Resolutions of the Board of Directors;

c) Organize the implementation of business plans and investment plans of the company;

d) Propose organizational structure, internal rules and regulations of the company;

e) Designate, dismiss, discharge from duty the company's managers, except for the positions within the competence of the Board of Directors;

f) Decide the salaries and other benefits of the company's employees, including the managers designated by the Director/General Director;

g) Hire employees;

h) Suggest plans for dividend payments or loss settlement;

i) Perform other rights and obligations prescribed by law, the company's charter, and Resolutions of the Board of Directors.

4. The Director/General Director shall run the company's everyday business in accordance with law, the company's charter, employment contract with the company, and Resolutions of the Board of Directors. If committing violations which cause damage to the company, the Director/General Director shall take legal responsibility and pay compensation for the company.

Salaries, remunerations, and other benefits of members of the Board of Directors, Director/General Director

1. The company is entitled to pay remunerations to Members of the Board of Directors, salaries to the Director/General Director and other managers according to the business outcome.

2. Unless otherwise prescribed by the company's charter, remunerations, salaries and other benefits of the Members of the Board of Directors, Director/General Director shall be paid as follows:

b) Members of the Board of Directors shall receive remunerations and bonuses. Remunerations are calculated according to the number of working days necessary for fulfilling the duties of Members of the Board of Directors and daily remuneration. The Board of Directors shall reach an agreement on estimated remuneration of each member. The total remuneration of the Board of Directors shall be decided by the General Meeting of Shareholders at the annual general meeting;

b) Members of the Board of Directors are entitled to have the cost of accommodation, meals, traveling, and other reasonable costs incurred during the performance of given duties reimbursed;

c) The Director/General Director shall receive salaries and bonuses. The Director/General Director's salaries and bonuses shall be decided by the Board of Directors.

Responsibilities of the company's managers

Members of the Board of Directors, Director/General Director, and other managers have the responsibilities to:

a) Perform given rights and obligations in accordance with regulations of law, the company's charter, and Resolutions of the General Meeting of Shareholders;

b) Perform given rights and obligations in a truthful, careful manner to ensure the company's legitimate interests;

c) Act in the best interest of the company and shareholders; do not use information, secrets, business opportunities of the company; do not misuse the position, power, or assets of the company for self-seeking purposes or serving the interest of other entities;

Control Board

Standards and conditions of Controllers

A Controller must:

a) be legally competent and not be banned from business administration and enterprise establishment as prescribed by this Law;

b) not be a spouse, birth parent, adoptive parent, birth child, adopted child, or sibling of any member of the Board of Directors, Director/General Director, or any other manager;

c) not hold managerial positions of the company. The Controller is not necessarily a shareholder or employee of the company;

Rights and obligations of the Control Board

The Control Board shall:

1. Supervise the Board of Directors, Director, or General Director managing and running the company.

2. Inspect the rationality, legitimacy, truthfulness, and prudence in business administration; the systematicness, consistency, and conformability of accounting works, statistical works, and the compilation of financial statements.

3. Inspect the sufficiency, legitimacy, and truthfulness of business outcome reports, annual and biannual financial statements of the company, management assessment report of the Board of Directors, and submit the inspection report at the annual general meeting.

4. Review, check, assess the effect and effectiveness of the internal control system, internal audit system, risk management and early warning system of the company.

5. Examine accounting books, accounting records and other documents of the company; managerial and administrative works of the company where necessary or under Resolutions of the General Meeting of Shareholders.

6. Propose changes, improvements to the organizational structure, mechanism for managing, supervising, and running the company's operation to the Board of Directors or the General Meeting of Shareholders.

7. Attend and discuss at meetings of the Board of Directors, General Meetings of Shareholders, and other meetings of the company.

Right to obtain information of the Control Board

1. Invitations, absentee ballots, and enclosed documents shall be sent to the Controllers at the same time and in the same manner as Members of the Board of Directors.

2. Resolutions and minutes of meetings of the Board of Directors and General Meetings of Shareholders shall be sent to the Controllers at the same time and in the same manner as shareholders and Members of the Board of Directors.

3. Reports of the Director/General Director submitted to the Board of Directors and other documents issued by the company shall be sent to the Controllers at the same time and in the same manner as Members of the Board of Directors.

4. Controllers are entitled to access documents of the company which are kept at the headquarter, branches, and other locations; entitled to enter working places of managers and employees of the company during working hours.

5. The Board of Directors, members of the Board of Directors, the Director/General Director, and other managers must provide sufficient, accurate, and timely information, documents about the management of the company at the request of members of the Control Board or the Control Board.

Responsibilities of Controllers

1. Comply with law, the company's charter, Resolutions of the General Meeting of Shareholders, and professional ethics while performing their rights and obligations.

2. Perform the given rights and obligations in a truthful, careful manner to ensure the company's legitimate interests;

3. Act in the best interest of the company and its shareholders; do not use information, secrets, business opportunities of the company; do not misuse the position, power, or assets of the company for self-seeking purposes or serving the interest of other entities;

4. Perform other rights and obligations prescribed in this Law and the company's charter.

5. The Controller that violates regulations and thus causes damage to the company or other persons shall take personal responsibility or pay compensation for such damage. All incomes and other interests of such Controller shall be returned to the company.

6. If a Controller is found committing violations while performing his/her given rights and obligations, the Board of Directors shall send a written notification to the Control Board, request the violator to stop the violations and take remedial measures.

Partnership

1. A partnership means an enterprise of which:

a) At least 02 partners are co-owner of the company who run a business together in a common name (hereinafter referred to as general partner). Apart from general partners, the company may have contributing partners;

b) General partners are individuals who are responsible for the company's obligations with all of their property;

c) Contributing partners are only liable for the company's debts up to the value of capital contributed to the company.

2. A partnership has its own legal status from the issuance date of the Certificate of Business registration.

3. Partnerships must not issue any kind of shares.

Contributing capital and issuing certificate of capital contribution

1. General partners and contributing partners shall fully and punctually contribute capital as committed.

2. The general partner who fails to fully and punctually contribute capital as committed shall pay compensation for any damage to the company.

3. If a contributing partner fails to fully and punctually contribute capital as committed, the deficit of capital is considered that partner's debt to the company; in this case such contributing partner may be removed from the company under a decision of the Board of partners.

4. As soon as capital is fully contributed, the partner shall be issued with the certificate of capital contribution. The certificate of capital contribution must contain the following information:

a) The enterprise's name, enterprise identification number, address of the headquarter;

b) The company's charter capital;

c) Name, permanent address, nationality, number of the people's identity card, passport or other legal personal certification of the partner and type of partner;

d) Value of contributed capital amount and type of assets used as contributed capital of partners;

e) Numbers and dates of issue of certificates of capital contribution;

f) Rights and obligations of holders of certificates of capital contribution;

g) Full names, signatures of holders of certificates of capital contribution and general partners.

5. If the certificate of capital contribution is lost or damaged or otherwise destroyed, the partner shall have it reissued by the company.

Assets of a partnership

Assets of a partnership include:

1. Contributed assets the ownership of which have been transferred to the company by members;

2. Created assets bearing the company's name;

3. Assets derived from business activities carried out by general partners on behalf of the company and from the business activities single-handedly carried out by general partners;

Restrictions on general partners

1. A general partner must not own a sole proprietorship or hold the position of the general partner of another partnership, unless otherwise agreed by other general partners.

2. General partners must not do the same business lines of the company, whether single-handedly or on behalf of another person, for self-seeking purposes or serving the interest of other entities;

3. A general partner must transfer part of or all of his/her stake to another person, unless otherwise agreed by other general partners.

Rights and obligations of general partners

1. Every general partner is entitled to:

a) Attend meetings, discuss, and vote on the company's issues; each general partner has a vote (or a number of votes prescribed by the company's charter);

b) Do the business lines of the company in the name of the company; negotiate, conclude contracts and agreements with the terms and conditions that are considered by the general partner most beneficial to the company;

c) Use the company's seal and assets to do the company's business lines. Any general partner who advances his/her own money to do the company's business is entitled to request the company to return the money, including both principal and interest at the market rate;

d) Request the company to compensate for the damage caused by the business operation if such damage is not at the partner's fault;

e) Request the company or another general partner to provide information about the company's performance; inspect the assets, accounting books, and other documents where necessary;

f) Receive distributed profits in proportion to the capital contribution or under agreement according to the company's charter;

h) If a general partner is dead or declared dead by the court, his/her heir shall enjoy the portion of the asset which the deceased partner shall be entitled to receive after his/her debt to the partnership has been paid. The heir may become a general partner if it is so approved by the Board of partners;

2. General partners have responsibilities to:

a) Manage and run the business in a truthful, careful manner to ensure the company's legitimate interests;

b) Manage and run the company's business in accordance with law, the company's charter, Resolutions of the Board of Partners; pay compensation for damage caused by failure to comply with regulations in this Point;

c) Not use the company's assets for self-seeking purposes or serving the interest of other entities;

d) Return the money, assets received, and pay compensation for damage to the company caused by receipt of money or assets from the company's business operation instead of giving it to the company, whether single-handedly, on behalf of the company, or on behalf of other persons;

e) Take joint responsibility for paying the remaining debts of the company if the company's assets are not sufficient to pay all its debts;

f) Bear a loss in proportion to their stakes in the company or under an agreement according to the company's charter in case the company suffers a loss;

g) Submit truthful and accurate monthly reports on his/her own performance; provide information about his/her owner performance to other partners at their request;

The Board of Partners

1. The Board of partners consists of all partners The Board of partners shall elect a general partner as the Chairperson of the Board of partner, who concurrently holds the position of Director/General Director of the company, unless otherwise prescribed by the company's charter.

2. General partners are entitled to request a meeting of the Board of partners to discuss and decide the company's business. The requesting partner shall prepare the meeting agenda and documents.

3. The Board of partners are entitled to decide every company's business.

The Board of Partners

1. The Board of partners consists of all partners The Board of partners shall elect a general partner as the Chairperson of the Board of partner, who concurrently holds the position of Director/General Director of the company, unless otherwise prescribed by the company's charter.

2. General partners are entitled to request a meeting of the Board of partners to discuss and decide the company's business. The requesting partner shall prepare the meeting agenda and documents.

3. The Board of partners are entitled to decide every company's business.

Convening meetings of Board of partners

1. The Chairperson of the Board of partners may convene a meeting of the Board of partners whenever it is deemed necessary or at the request of general partners. If the Chairperson of the Board of partners fails to convene a meeting at the request of a general partner, such partner shall convene the meeting.

2. The invitation to the meeting may be made in writing, by phone, fax, or another electronic medium. The invitation must specify the purposes, requirements, contents, agenda, location of the meeting, and name of the partner that request the meeting.

3. The Chairperson of the Board of convening partner shall chair the meeting. Every meeting of the Board of partners must be recorded into the minutes. The minutes must contain:

a) The enterprise's name, enterprise identification number, address of the headquarter;

b) Purposes, agenda, and contents of the meeting;

c) Time and location of the meeting;

d) Full names of the chair and attending partners;

e) Opinions of attending partners;

f) The Resolutions ratified, number of partners that cast affirmative votes, and basic contents of such Resolutions;

g) Full names and signatures of attending partners.

Running a partnership's business

1. General partners are entitled to act as the company's legal representatives and run the company's everyday business.

2. While running the company's business, general partners shall hold various positions of managers and controllers.

When some or all general partners does certain business works, decisions shall be ratified under the majority rule.

The company is not responsible for any work done by a general partner beyond the company's scope of business, unless such work is accepted by other partners.

3. The company may open one or some bank accounts. The Board of partners shall authorize a partner to deposit and withdraw money from such accounts.

4. The Chairperson of the Board of partners, the Director/General Director has the duties:

a) Run the company's everyday business as general partners;

b) Convene and organize meetings of the Board of partners; sign Resolutions of the Board of partners;

c) Give tasks and cooperate with other general partners in doing business;

d) Arrange and keep accounting books, invoices, and other documents of the company in accordance with law;

e) Represent the company in the relationship with regulatory bodies; represent the company as defendant or plaintiff in lawsuits, commercial disputes, or other disputes;

Termination of general partner's status

The general partner's status shall be terminated if the general partner:

a) Voluntarily withdraws capital from the company;

b) Dies, is declared missing, or legally incompetent by the court;

c) Is removed from the company;

d) Other cases prescribed by the company's charter.

PRIVATE ENTERPRISES

Private enterprises

1. A private enterprise is an enterprise owned by an individual who is responsible for its operation with all of his/her property.

2. Private enterprises must not issue any kind of shares.

3. Each individual may establish only one private enterprise . The owner of a private enterprise must not concurrently be a partner of a partnership.

4. Private enterprises must not contribute capital to the establishment, buy shares or stakes in partnerships, limited liability companies, or joint-stock companies.

Owner's capital

1. The capital of owner of a private enterprise is registered by the owner himself)herself. The private enterprise owner must register the exact amount of capital in the local currencies, a convertible currency, gold, or other assets; if capital is in the form of other assets, the type, quantity, and remaining value of each type of assets must be specified.

2. All capital and assets, including loan capital and leased assets used for the company's business operation, must be recorded in the company's accounting books and financial statements as prescribed by law.

3. During the operation, the owner of the private enterprise may increase or increase his/her capital investment in the company's business operation. The increase or decrease in the owner's capital must be recorded in accounting books.

Business management

1. The owner of the private enterprise has the absolute discretion as to the company's business operation, the use of post-tax profit, and shall fulfill other financial obligations as prescribed by law.

2. The owner may directly or hire another person to manage the business operation. When hiring another person as the Director, the owner is still responsible for every business operation of the company.

3. The owner of the private enterprise is the company's legal representative.

Company leasing

The owner of the private enterprise is entitled to lease out his/her entire company, provided a written notification enclosed with a notarized copy of the lease contract is sent to the business registration authority and tax authority. In this case, the private enterprise 's owner is still legally responsible as the enterprise's owner. The rights and obligations or the owner and the lessee to the company's business operation shall be specified in the lease contract.

Selling company

1. The private enterprise 's owner is entitled to sell his/her company to another person.

2. After selling the company, the private enterprise 's owner is still responsible for the company's debts and other liabilities which are incurred before the handover date, unless otherwise agreed among the buyer, the seller, and the creditors.

3. The buyer and seller shall comply with regulations of law on labor.

4. The buyer shall register a change of the private enterprise 's owner in accordance with this Law.

GROUPS OF COMPANIES

Group of companies

1. A group of companies is a combination of companies which have long-term interrelations in terms of economic benefits, technology, market and other business services.

2. Groups of companies include:

a) Parent company - subsidiary company;

b) Economic conglomerate;

Parent company and subsidiaries

1. A company is considered parent company of another company if the former company:

a) Owns more than 50% of charter capital or total ordinary shares of the other company;

b) Is entitle to directly or indirectly decide the designation of a majority of or all of Members of the Board of Directors, the Director/General Director of the other company;

c) Is entitled to decide amendments to the other company's charter.

2. Subsidiaries must not contribute capital to or buy shares of the parent company. Subsidiaries of the same parent company must not contribute capital or buy shares of each other for the purpose of cross ownership.

Economic conglomerates

Economic conglomerate is a large group of companies.

RESTRUCTURING, DISSOLUTION, AND BANKRUPTCY OF ENTERPRISES

Total Division

1. A limited liability company with two or more members or joint-stock company may divide shareholders/members, and assets of the company (hereinafter referred to as transferor company) to establish two new companies or more (hereinafter referred to as transferee company) in one of the following cases:

a) Part of stakes/shares of members/shareholders and an amount of assets proportional to the value of stakes/shares are transferred to the transferee companies according to their holding in the transferor company and corresponding to the value of assets transferred to the transferee companies;

b) All of stakes/shares of one or some members/shareholders and an amount of assets proportional to the value of stakes/shares are transferred to the transferee enterprises;

2. Procedures for total division of a limited liability company with two or more members or joint-stock company:

a) The Board of members, the owner, or the General Meeting of Shareholders of the transferor company shall ratify the Resolution on the total division in accordance with regulations of law and the company's charter. The Resolution on total division must contain basic information including the transferor company's name, headquarter addresses, names of transferee companies; rules, method, and procedures for asset division; employment plan; method, time limit, and procedures for transferring the transferor company's stakes, shares, bonds to transferee companies; rules for fulfillment of the transferor company's obligations; time limit for division.

b) Members, the owner, or shareholders of each of the transferee companies shall ratify its charter, elect or designate the Chairperson of the Board of members, the company's President, the Board of Directors, Director/General Director, and apply for business registration in accordance with regulations of law.

3. The number of members, shareholders, their holding of stakes/shares, the quantity of shareholders and charter capital of the transferee companies are corresponding to the method of dividing, transferring stakes/shares of the transferor company to the transferee companies.

4. The transferor company shall cease to exist after the transferee companies are issued with their Certificates of Business registration. Transferee companies are jointly responsible for the unpaid debts, employment contracts, and other liabilities of the transferor company, or reach agreements with the creditors, customers, and employees to decide on one of the companies to settle such obligations.

Partial Division

1. A limited liability company with two or more members or joint-stock company may be partially divided by transferring part of its existing assets, rights and obligations (hereinafter referred to as transferor company) to establish one or some new limited liability companies or joint-stock companies (hereinafter referred to as transferee companies) without terminating the existence of the transferor company.

2. Partial division may be carried out using one of the following methods:

a) Part of stakes/shares of members/shareholders and an amount of assets proportional to the value of stakes/shares are transferred to the transferee companies according to their holding in the transferor company and corresponding to the value of assets transferred to the transferee companies;

b) All of stakes/shares of one or some members/shareholders and an amount of assets proportional to the value of their stakes/shares are transferred to the transferee companies;

3. The transferor company shall register a change to charter capital and a number of members, which are proportional to the decrease in stakes/shares and quantity of members, at the same time with the business registration of transferee companies.

4. Procedures for partial division of a limited liability company with two or more members or a joint-stock company:

a) The Board of members, the owner, or the General Meeting of Shareholders of the transferor company shall ratify the Resolution on the partial division in accordance with this Law and the company's charter. The Resolution on partial division must contain basic information including the transferor company's name, headquarter addresses, names of transferee companies; employment plan; division method; the value of assets, rights and obligations transferred from the transferor company to the transferee companies; time limit for the division.

b) Members, the owner, or shareholders of each of the transferee companies shall ratify its charter, elect or designate Chairpersons of the Board of members, the company's President, the Board of Directors, Director/General Director, and apply for business registration in accordance with this Law. In this case, the application for enterprise registration must be enclosed with the Resolution on partial division mentioned in Point a of this Clause.

5. After business registration, the transferor company and transferee companies are jointly responsible for the unpaid debts, employment contracts, and other liabilities of the transferor company, unless otherwise agreed among the transferor company, transferee companies, the transferor company's creditors, customers, and employees.

Corporate Amalgamation

1. Two or some companies (hereinafter referred to as consolidating companies) may consolidate into a new company (hereinafter referred to as consolidated company). After that, consolidating companies shall cease to exist.

2. Procedures for consolidation:

a) The consolidating companies prepare the consolidation contract. The consolidation contract must contain the consolidating companies' names, headquarter addresses; the consolidated company's name and headquarter address; procedures and conditions for consolidation; employment plan; time limit and procedures for transferring assets, stakes, shares, bonds of the consolidating companies to the consolidated company; time limit for consolidation; draft charter of the consolidated company;

b) Members, the owner, or shareholders of the consolidating companies shall ratify the consolidation contract, the consolidated company's charter, elect or designate Chairpersons of the Board of members, the company's President, the Board of Directors, Director/General Director of the consolidated company, and apply for business registration in accordance with this Law.

3. After business registration, the consolidating companies shall cease to exist; the consolidated company shall inherit the lawful rights and interests as well as unpaid debts, employment contract, and other liabilities of the consolidating companies.

Acquisition

1. One or some companies (hereinafter referred to as acquired companies) may be merged into another company (hereinafter referred to as the acquirer) by transferring all assets, legitimate rights, obligations, and interests to the acquirer. After that, the acquired companies shall cease to exist.

2. Procedures for acquisition:

a) Relevant companies shall prepare the acquisition contract and draft the charter of the acquirer. The acquisition contract must contain the acquirer's names, headquarter addresses; the acquired company's name and headquarter address; procedures and conditions for acquisition; employment plan; time limit and procedures for transferring assets, stakes, shares, bonds of the consolidating companies to the acquirer; time limit for acquisition;

b) Members, the owners, or shareholders of each of relevant companies shall ratify the acquisition contract, the charter of the acquirer, and apply for registration of the acquirer as prescribed by this Law.

c) After business registration, the acquired companies shall cease to exist; the acquirer shall inherit the lawful rights and interests as well as unpaid debts, employment contract, and other liabilities of the acquired companies.

Converting a limited liability company with two or more members into a joint-stock company

1. A limited liability company with two or more members may be converted into a joint-stock company in one of the following manners:

a) Conversion into a joint-stock company without raising capital from other entities, without selling stakes to other entities;

b) Conversion into a joint-stock company by raising capital from other entities;

c) Conversion into a joint-stock company by selling part of or all of the stakes to one or some other entities;

2. The converted company obviously inherits all of the lawful rights and interests, debts including tax debts, employment contracts, and other obligations of the old company.

Converting a joint-stock company into a one-member limited liability company

1. A joint-stock company may be converted into a one-member limited liability company in one of the following manners:

a) A shareholder receives the transfer of all shares and stakes of all other shareholders;

b) An organization or individual other than a shareholder receives the transfer of all shares of all of the company's shareholders;

2. The converted company obviously inherits all of the lawful rights and interests, debts including tax debts, employment contracts, and other obligations of the old company.

Converting a joint-stock company into a multi-member limited liability company with two or more members

1. A joint-stock company may be converted into a multi-member limited liability company with two or more members in one of the following manners:

a) Conversion into a limited liability company with two or more members without raising additional capital or transferring shares to other entities;

b) Conversion into a limited liability company with two or more members together with raising capital from other entities;

c) Conversion into a limited liability company with two or more members together with transferring part of or all of the shares to other organizations and individuals that contribute capital;

2. The converted company obviously inherits all of the lawful rights and interests, debts including tax debts, employment contracts, and other obligations of the old company.

Converting a private enterprise into a limited liability company with two or more members

A private enterprise may be converted into a limited liability company with two or more members under a decision of the private enterprise 's owner if all of the following conditions are satisfied:

a) The private enterprise 's owner is the owner (if the private enterprise is converted into one-member limited liability company under the ownership of an individual) or member (if the private enterprise is converted into a multi-member limited liability company with two or more members) of the limited liability company with two or more members;

b) The private enterprise 's owner makes a written commitment to take personal responsibility for all unpaid debts of the private enterprise with all of his/her property and to settle the debts when they are due;

c) The private enterprise 's owner has a written agreement with parties of unfinished contracts that the new limited liability company with two or more members will take over such contracts;

d) The private enterprise 's owner makes a written commitment or agreement with other capital contributors to employ the existing employees of the private enterprise.

Cases of and conditions for dissolution

1. An enterprise shall be dissolved in the following cases:

a) The operation period written in the company's charter expires without a decision on extension;

b) The dissolution is decided by the owner of the private enterprise , by all general partners of the partnership, by the Board of members or owner of the limited liability company with two or more members, or insurance the General Meeting of Shareholders of the joint-stock company;

c) The company fails to maintain the minimum number of members prescribed by this Law for 06 consecutive months without following procedures for business conversion;

d) The Certificate of Business registration is revoked.

2. The enterprise shall only be dissolved if all debts and liabilities can be settled and the enterprise is involved in any dispute at a court or arbitral tribunal.

Banned activities as from issuance of decision on dissolution

From the issuance of the decision on dissolution, the enterprise and its manager are prohibited to:

a) Hide, illegally liquidate assets;

b) Renounce or reduce the right to claim debts;

c) Convert unsecured debts into debts secured on the enterprise's assets;

d) Sign new contracts, except for those serving the enterprise's dissolution;

e) Mortgage, pledge, give, lease out assets;

f) Terminate effective contracts;

g) Raise capital in any shape or form.

Shut down of branches and representative offices

1. A branch or representative office of an enterprise shall be terminated under a decision of the enterprise or a decision to revoke the Certificate of registration of branch or representative office issued by a competent authority

2. Documents for Shut down of a branch or representative office includes:

a) The decision of the enterprise to shut down the branch or representative office, or the decision to revoke the Certificate of registration of branch or representative office issued by a competent authority;

b) The list of creditors and outstanding debts, including tax debts, of the branch and outstanding social insurance contributions;

c) The list of employees and their corresponding benefits;

d) The Certificate of registration of the branch or representative office;

e) The seal of the branch or representative office (if any).

3. The enterprise's legal representative and the head of the shut down branch or representative office are jointly responsible for the truthfulness and accuracy of the said documents.

4. The enterprise whose branch is shut down is responsible for the execution of contracts, payment of debts, including tax debts, of the branch, keep employing the branch's employees or provide them with adequate benefits.

Bankruptcy

Regulations of law on bankruptcy shall apply to the bankruptcy of enterprises.

CONCLUSION

Thank you again for downloading this book on *"COMPANY LAW: Mastering Essential Legal Terms Explained About Limited Liability Companies, Joint-Stock Companies, Partnership, Private Enterprises, And Groups of Companies!"* and reading all the way to the end. I'm extremely grateful.

If you know of anyone else who may benefit from the informative legal words presented in this book, please help me inform them of this book. I would greatly appreciate it.

Finally, if you enjoyed this book and feel that it has added value to your study or career in any way, please take a couple of minutes to share your thoughts and post a REVIEW on Amazon. Your feedback will help me to continue to write the kind of Kindle books that helps you get results. Furthermore, if you write a simple REVIEW with positive words for this book on Amazon, you can help hundreds or perhaps thousands of other readers who may want to enhance their legal understanding have a chance getting what they need. Like you, they worked hard for every penny they spend on books. With the information and recommendation you provide, they would be more likely to take action right away. We really look forward to reading your review.

Thanks again for your support and good luck!

If you enjoy my book, please write a POSITIVE REVIEW on amazon.

-- Dr. Peter Johnson --

COMPANY LAW: Mastering Essential Legal Terms Explained About Limited Liability Companies, Joint-Stock Companies, Partnership, Private Enterprises, And Groups of Companies!

https://www.amazon.com/dp/B07P2PRVMJ

INVESTMENT LAW: Essential Legal Terms Explained You Need To Know About Law On Investment!

https://www.amazon.com/dp/B07P79D925

LABOR LAW: Essential Legal Terms Explained You Need To Know About Law On Labor!

https://www.amazon.com/dp/B07PFD2CML

CIVIL LAW: Mastering Essential Legal Terms Explained About Civil Rights, Guardianship, Civil Transactions, Civil Obligations, Civil Liability, Civil Contracts And Civil Procedure!

https://www.amazon.com/dp/B07P5GS8LD

Legal Vocabulary In Use: Master 600+ Essential Legal Terms And Phrases Explained In 10 Minutes A Day

http://www.amazon.com/dp/B01L0FKXPU

Civil Law Vocabulary In Use: Master 350+ Essential Civil Law Terms And Phrases Explained With Examples In 10 Minutes A Day.

https://www.amazon.com/dp/B0781TQWGV

Criminal Law Vocabulary In Use: Master 400+ Essential Criminal Law Terms And Phrases Explained With Examples In 10 Minutes A Day.

https://www.amazon.com/dp/B078KLR51Z

Administrative And Tax Law In Use : Master 300+ Administrative And Tax Law Terms And Phrases Explained With Examples In 10 Minutes A Day.

https://www.amazon.com/dp/B07JMD546J

Productivity Secrets For Students: The Ultimate Guide To Improve Your Mental Concentration, Kill Procrastination, Boost Memory And Maximize Productivity In Study

http://www.amazon.com/dp/B01JS52UT6

Shortcut To Ielts Writing: The Ultimate Guide To Immediately Increase Your Ielts Writing Scores

http://www.amazon.com/dp/B01JV7EQGG